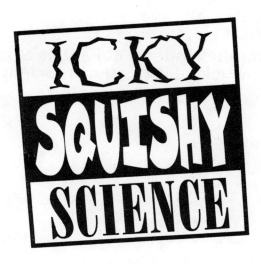

ICKY SQUISHY SCIENCE

Sandra Markle

Illustrated by Cecile Schoberle

Hyperion Paperbacks for Children
New York

For the students at Paideia School
who love icky, squishy science
—S. M.

First Hyperion Paperback edition 1996
Text ©1996 by Sandra Markle.
Illustrations © 1996 by Cecile Schoberle.

A library edition of *Icky, Squishy Science* is also available.

Printed in the United States of America.

First Edition
1 3 5 7 9 10 8 6 4 2

The text for this book is set in 13-point Candida.
Designed by Lara S. Demberg.

Library of Congress Cataloging-in-Publication Data

Markle, Sandra.
Icky, squishy science / Sandra Markle ; illustrated by Cecile
Schoberle.
p.   cm.
Summary: Details numerous science experiments
which can be done at home, explains the various scientific
phenomena involved, and suggests further experiments.
ISBN 0-7868-2177-9 (lib. bdg.)—0-7868-1087-4 (pbk.)
1. Science—Experiments—Juvenile literature. 2. Science—
Experiments—Methodology—Juvenile literature. 3. Scientific
recreations—Juvenile literature. [1. Science—Experiments.
2. Experiments. 3. Scientific recreations.] I. Schoberle, Cecile,
ill. II. Title.
Q164M2734   1996
507'.8—dc20   95-46173

Contents

This book is guaranteed to have you foaming at the mouth over science—for real. And don't bother to wash your hands before you start experimenting. You'll soon be squeezing plaster, poking dead fish, and petting earthworms. If that's not icky enough for you, then you should know you'll be eating worms, too. If you've never before smashed a ripe banana with your fist, you're about to get your chance. You'll also be blowing up marshmallows, using your breath to make water change color, turning a chicken bone rubbery, and lots more disgusting stuff—all for the sake of science.

So if you're ready—and brave enough—don't wait another second to get started. You'll just need materials you can find at home or buy cheaply at a grocery store, gardening store, or hardware store. Along the way, you'll also have opportunities to develop your own experiments. How icky and squishy you make them is up to you, providing you check out your plans first with an adult. But to help you get started, here are steps you can work through to tackle any problem-solving situation.

1) Think about everything you already know about the problem. What did you learn by doing an earlier investigation? Is there anything you could look up if you visited the library?
2) Brainstorm possible solutions. Limit yourself to no more than fifteen minutes and write down every idea that comes into your head.
3) Analyze your list of possible solutions. Be critical

as you consider reasons why your ideas might not work. Choose the one idea you think will have the best chance of being successful. Be sure to check with an adult that what you want to try will be safe for you.

4) Test your solution. If you are setting up an experiment, be sure that everything is identical except the one thing you want to change. For example, in the activity on page 11, you'll be testing to see how adding salt affects how quickly plaster of Paris hardens. Everything about the test should be identical except adding salt to the water. Every test should also be repeated at least three times to be sure the results are what is likely to happen every time.

5) Always analyze the results of your test. Did your idea work? From what you discovered, is there anything else you could try that might work even better?

Remember

- Don't do any activity that requires you to use a stove or a microwave without an adult partner.
- Clean up the work area after you finish your activity.
- Recycle materials whenever possible.
- Have fun!

Foam at the Mouth

It's icky. It's disgusting. It's fun. Try it.

You'll need:
- **toothbrush**
- **toothpaste (kind with baking soda)**
- **carbonated soft drink or carbonated mineral water**

Be sure to do this investigation at the bathroom sink. Put toothpaste on your toothbrush and brush away. Now, before you spit, take a drink of the carbonated drink. Don't swallow. Swish the drink around inside your mouth.

Feel the bubbles? Lean over the sink and open your mouth just a little. Foam will ooze out. If you can look in the mirror without making a mess, don't miss the chance to see yourself. When you're tired of foaming at the mouth, spit out as much foam as possible and rinse your mouth out with water.

Wondering what caused all the foam? John Malone of the American Dental Association explained that it starts with the toothpaste itself. Toothpaste contains sodium lauryl sulfate, a type of soap. When you brush, this gets mixed with saliva, the digestive juice that's naturally in

1

your mouth. Then the friction of brushing, like rubbing your wet, soapy hands together, makes the sodium lauryl sulfate and saliva produce bubbles. The bubbles help lift bits of food sticking to your teeth and carry them away.

But toothpaste produces only very tiny bubbles. The carbonated drink contains bigger bubbles— bubbles of carbon dioxide gas, the same gas you breathe out and that your body gives off as waste. The carbonated gas bubbles mix with the toothpaste, greatly increasing the amount of foam. So now instead of a little suds, you've got a whole mouthful of the stuff and it's oozing out as if you're a pot boiling over.

The foam also lasts a long time because toothpaste contains another ingredient called *glycerin* that slows down how quickly water is lost. So the bubbles don't burst immediately upon coming in contact with the air. The old foam lasts while even more is produced. This pushes the old foam out of your mouth to slip over your lips and slide down your chin.

This activity won't work with a tooth gel, though. Gels don't contain sodium lauryl sulfate, the soap that gets the action started.

Toothpaste Once Contained *Crab Eyes?*

People have been mixing up toothpaste since ancient times. Early toothpastes were nothing like the ones used today, though. Historical records show that the ancient Romans sometimes used toothpastes made of honey, blood, charcoal, oils, and ground-up crab eyes. Now, that's really icky!

One of the most common early toothpastes was powdered marble. Toothpaste still contains powdered minerals, such as finely ground chalk. This mildly abrasive material helps rub away a film called *plaque* that coats the teeth. Plaque is a sticky material that contains a kind of bacteria. This bacteria can cause cavities and gum disease.

Today's toothpaste also contains xanthan gum that makes it thick enough to squeeze out of the tube onto your toothbrush. Flavoring and an artificial sweetener makes toothpaste taste good enough that you're willing to put it in your mouth. Some toothpastes also contain fluoride, a chemical that helps reduce tooth decay by hardening the outer enamel layer of the teeth.

Go Ahead and Spit

How far can you spit? Check it out. Go outdoors where it's paved, check that no one is in the way, work up a squishy mouthful, and let it fly. Measure how far from your feet your spit landed. Do you think you could hit a target? Set a paper or plastic cup a little closer than you were able to spit. Then work up another glob of spit—aim and fire.

Even at your spitting best, though, you're not likely to be a match for the champ—the archer fish (*Toxotes jaculator*). Full grown archer fish have been known to spit water-drops as far as one and a half meters (about five feet). The fish spits by suddenly compressing its gill covers, forcing water through a tiny tube formed by its tongue and the inside of its mouth. But an archer fish doesn't spit just for the fun of it. These freshwater fish hang around just below the surface of the water watching for insects. When an unsuspecting bug comes close, the archer fish spits, propelling the water-drop out of the lake. With any luck, an insect is struck by this water bullet and drops into the lake. Then the archer fish can gulp down a buggy meal.

Since you're not likely to want to knock bugs out of the air, you're probably wondering what good is spit. Try this to find out.

You'll need:
- **clean, dry paper towel**
- **soda cracker**
- **piece of waxed paper**

First, wash and dry your hands. Then stick your tongue out and use the paper towel to blot it. Place the soda cracker on your nearly dry tongue. Keep your tongue stuck out while you count from one to six. Can you taste the soda cracker? You won't if your tongue stays dry.

Pull your tongue back into your mouth, but don't chew. Count to six again. Spit gushes into your mouth. Taste the cracker now? You should.

Okay, now spit the soft cracker out on the piece of waxed paper and take a close look. Touch the mush, too. The cracker has broken down into tiny particles suspended in liquid—your spit. Spit *is* saliva, a natural juice produced by your body. Its job is to soften food and break it apart into tiny particles—tiny enough to get into the very tiny taste buds on your tongue.

Examine your tongue in the mirror. Those bumps contain taste buds, special egg-shaped spots with an opening at the top. But the openings to the taste buds are very small. Only liquids, like things you drink and saliva, can pass through. Inside each taste bud, there are tiny, taste-sensitive parts that send messages to your brain. And when your brain analyzes these messages you're able to tell if something is sweet, sour, salty, or bitter. That happens almost instantly, once the things you eat or drink get inside the taste buds.

Now, here's another reason why spit is good. Work up a

glob of spit in your mouth. Then push it out with your tongue, letting it drip down your chin. Which feels cooler—the part of your face that's wet or the part that's dry?

The part of your face that's wet with drool should feel cooler. Your saliva is mainly water that when warmed by your body-heat changes to a gas and moves into the air. This process is called *evaporation*. The part of your skin where evaporation occurred feels cooler because it used up heat energy. Although you're not likely to use your spit to cool off, some animals do. Kangaroo rats, for example, drool—letting spit ooze over their chin and down their throat to cool off when they get overheated.

Bend a Bone

Imagine being able to bend a bone! You can make a hard chicken bone turn rubbery with a little help from science.

You'll need:
- **drinking glass**
- **chicken wing bone (use a cooked chicken wing)**
- **vinegar**

You'll need help from an adult partner for this activity.

The chicken wing is made up of two parts: 1) short part with a single bone; 2) triangular-shaped tip with two smaller bones.

Chicken Wing Bone

Use the thinnest bone from the wing tip. Have an adult separate the two sections of a cooked chicken wing. Peel the skin and meat off the bone. Wash off the bone. Place one end on the kitchen counter and push down gently on the other end. The bone doesn't bend because it's strengthened with a hard material called *calcium carbonate*. You may be surprised to learn that you can dissolve or break down this hard material using another kind of matter called an *acid*.

There are many different kinds of acids, some weak and some strong. Acids share the same special characteristics when dissolved in water: a sour taste, the ability to break down certain materials like calcium carbonate and metals, and the ability to conduct electricity. It's weak acids in foods, like lemons, that make them taste sour. It's a weak form of acid in your stomach that helps break down the foods you eat. For this activity, you'll use a weak acid—vinegar. Pour enough vinegar into the glass to cover the chicken bone. Look closely. You'll see tiny bubbles on the bone. That's the acid already at work attacking the calcium carbonate material in the bone.

After two days, drain the glass and add fresh vinegar. On the fourth day, test the bone again by placing one end on the counter and gently pressing down on the other end. If the bone doesn't bend easily, return it to the vinegar bath. Continue checking the bone at two-day intervals until it bends easily. How long will it take for hard bone to turn rubbery? That depends on how thick the bone is and how much calcium carbonate material has to be dissolved. But it should bend easily within a week.

Dr. Sidney Crow of the biology department at Georgia State University explains that even after the calcium carbonate is removed, the weak acid will not be able to break down the rubbery material—which maintains the shape of the bone.

Squeeze a Rock Sculpture

Now get ready to plunge your hands into something really messy. It'll be squishy at first, but in just a little while, the stuff will turn rock hard. Wondering how this is possible? Don't miss the scientific explanation of what makes this amazing transformation happen.

You'll need:
- **plaster of Paris powder**
- **self-sealing plastic bag**
- **water**
- **measuring cup**
- **measuring spoons**
- **waxed paper**

Pour a cup of plaster of Paris powder into the bag. Pour in a half cup of water. Stick one hand into the bag and squeeze to mix. Repeat, adding water a tablespoon at a time until the powder is transformed into a material that feels and looks a lot like thick mashed potatoes. Next, grab a handful of the stuff and shape it into a work of art. Simple shapes are best. Then set your sculpture on a piece of waxed paper and wait. Gradually, the soft plaster will become rock hard.

Does the plaster harden because it's drying out? To find out, make a second sculpture but set this one underwater in a bowl or the sink. Surprise! It will become rock hard, too.

Plaster of Paris is actually a powdered rock called *gypsum*. Everything in the universe is made up of tiny building blocks called molecules. Gypsum is made up of molecules of a hard material and water. To create plaster of Paris powder, the gypsum is heated hot enough to make most of the water molecules evaporate. Then the hard material is crushed into a powder. Adding water to plaster of Paris powder is like gluing the molecules back together. The water molecules connect with molecules of the hard material, making them stick together. And when all the molecules are tightly bonded once again, the gypsum returns to its rock-hard form. What makes this whole process so useful is that it's a way to briefly make a rock pliable so it can be shaped without chiseling and chipping. Then it hardens, maintaining whatever shape you gave it.

So why is the plaster called plaster of Paris? When people first discovered this process for sculpting with gypsum, the gypsum came from Montmartre in Paris, France.

Can You Make Plaster of Paris Harden Faster?

Hate to wait? Then you'll want your plaster of Paris sculpture to harden even faster. You can do it, too, with a little help from science. Just follow the directions to find out how.

You'll need:
- **1 1/2 teaspoons salt**
- **2 self-sealing plastic sandwich bags**
- **waxed paper**
- **permanent marker**
- **measuring spoon**
- **measuring cup**
- **plaster of Paris powder**
- **penny**

Mark an **X** on one bag. Pour one-fourth cup cool tap water into each bag. Add one-fourth teaspoon of salt to the **X** bag. Seal and shake both bags while you count to twenty. It's important to treat the freshwater bag exactly as you do the saltwater bag. That way you'll know that any difference you observe between what happens to the plaster in the two bags was caused by the salt.

Next, add a fourth cup of plaster powder to each bag, seal, and squeeze to mix. Continue adding plaster powder—one tablespoon at a time—until the dough is like thick mashed potatoes. Roll three nearly identical plaster balls from the dough in each bag. Place the plaster balls made with salt water in one line on the waxed paper and the freshwater plaster balls in another line. Set a penny next to those made with salt water.

After one minute, press on the balls in each row. Is one harder than another? Are there any other differences? Write down your observations.

Keep checking at one-minute intervals for five minutes or until one plaster ball is completely hard. Which hardened first? It should be the plaster made with salt water.

Experts at the UNI-C, Danish Computing Centre for Research and Education, explain that adding salt makes the plaster harden faster because the salt helps the plaster molecules combine with the water molecules more quickly. Remember, the plaster powder was originally made by driving off the water molecules. So the faster water molecules reconnect with the plaster molecules, the faster the plaster turns back into its natural rock-hard form.

Of course, you should repeat this test at least two more times to be sure that the results you observed are what's likely to happen every time.

Boning Up on Sculpture

Okay, now it's time to plaster some old bones. That's the way plaster of Paris is used by a *paleontologist*, a scientist that studies prehistoric life. Al Sanders, a paleontologist at the Charleston Museum in Charleston, South Carolina, supplied these directions.

1) Make a fossil jacket

Fossil bones are the remains of ancient animals. Hundreds of thousands of years ago, minerals soaked into the animal's bones and filled in tiny spaces. These hardened so when the real bone was gone, the rock remained in the shape of the bone. Fossils are often found in deserts and other places where it isn't easy to work and study. So paleontologists want to move the fossils to a laboratory. The problem is to protect the bones while they're being transported. And it's important to keep a group of fossil bones in the same position they were found. This helps the paleontologist who will later try to reconstruct the animal's skeleton.

First, create a simulated fossil site by filling a shoe box half full of sand or soil, arranging several dry chicken bones, and pouring on more material to bury them. Next dig the bones out slowly, the way a scientist would by removing the sand or soil a little at a time and then using a paintbrush to clean off the upper surface of the bones. Next, carefully dig a trench under the bones, leaving only the ends anchored in the soil.

Wet newspaper strips and wrap this softened paper around the bones. The wet paper prevents the plaster from sticking to any exposed surface of the bone. Be sure to cover the ends, too. Cover the bones with burlap (available at stores that sell cloth by the yard). Then mix up plaster of Paris and coat the bones with this until it forms a package. When the plaster is completely dry, the package can be dug out of the soil without damaging the bones or separating the group.

Back in the laboratory, the paleontologists can chip away the plaster and remove the wrappings to expose the bones.

2) Make a plaster cast of a fossil

Making a plaster cast makes it possible for paleontologists to display and study the plaster cast while the actual fossil remains safely stored away. To do this, scientists first spread latex, a rubbery material, on the fossil to make a mold. The mold is two halves that fit tightly together. The mold is filled with plaster of Paris. When the plaster hardens, the mold is opened and the cast is removed. It's an exact duplicate in shape, size, and form of the original fossil.

While a mold cast is difficult to make, you can easily make another kind of cast—the kind used to preserve fossil footprints. To make a cast of a footprint, first smooth out the surface of the soil or sand in your shoe box. Step in it hard enough to make an imprint at least five centimeters (about two inches) deep. Mix up enough plaster of Paris to fill your footprint and let it dry. Lift out the cast of your footprint and brush off any loose dirt.

Did You Know that a Cockroach Could Eat Your Homework?

Your teacher may not believe this excuse, but it could really happen. Cockroaches will eat almost anything. These hardy critters have mouth parts capable of chewing either hard or soft materials. The U.S. Department of Agriculture reports cockroaches will eat grease spots off kitchen walls and the starch on wallpaper—they will even eat the starch that makes up the glue on postage stamps. Cockroaches have also been known to chew on tennis shoes, seeking the salts left by sweaty feet. Hungry cockroaches will even nibble on each other, chewing off any antennae or legs they can grab. Now, that's really icky!

Not all cockroaches are small, either. The Madagascar hissing cockroach can get as big as a mouse. What does this giant cockroach eat? Anything it wants—almost.

WARNING:
This Is Disgusting!

It's time to examine a dead fish. If one hasn't died recently in your aquarium, you can buy one at the grocery store or fish market. Just be sure to get one that has scales. A few kinds, such as catfish, don't have any scales. Then put on rubber gloves—the kind you can buy at grocery stores or hardware stores—and you're ready to begin.

Look at the fish's shape—tapered at either end and flattened in the middle. It's called *streamlining* and helps the fish slip through the water with little resistance. Feel the fish's fins. Move them to see how they can change shape and position. When the fish was alive, it propelled itself forward mainly by moving its tail and tail fin from side to side. The single fins above and below its body helped keep the fish from rolling over. The paired fins on either side helped it to steer itself through the water.

Stroke the fish's body. Does it feel slimy? It should. Fish just naturally have a slimy coat to help them slip through the water and to protect them from disease-causing organisms. Take a close look at the scales. Use a magnifying glass if you have one. The scales usually overlap like the shingles on a roof. This shields the fish's body and also helps streamline it. Different kinds of fish have scales of different shapes. What shape are your fish's scales? Look for a line running from the fish's head to its tail. This is the lateral line, a sort of liquid-filled tube running under the skin with little openings to the surface. When moving water bends tiny hairs inside these tubes, signals go to the brain. This alerts the fish to moving prey or enemies that are altering the natural currents in the water.

Check out the fish's eyes, too. There isn't a lid, so a fish can't blink or wink or shut its eyes. See the little nostrils in front of the eyes? These are for detecting smells only and not for breathing. You may be surprised to learn that odors can be carried by water. Many fish use smell to detect prey hiding in murky water or buried under the sandy sea bottom.

The large bony flap behind the eyes is called the *operculum* and it covers the gills. Lift it and peek inside. If the gills haven't been removed you'll see them. These body parts are where oxygen and carbon dioxide are exchanged, allowing a fish to breathe.

Why Does a Dead Fish Float?

Did you ever discover a dead body floating belly-up in water?

Before you shout no! stop and think. Did you ever have a pet goldfish that died? Dead fish usually float. Wonder why? This experiment will let you find out.

You'll need:
- **self-sealing plastic sandwich bag**
- **1 package dry yeast granules (1 tablespoon)**
- **1/2 teaspoon sugar**
- **1/4 cup warm water**
- **teacup or glass**
- **spoon**
- **aquarium or clear plastic storage box**
- **rock**

WATER   YEAST   SUGAR

Fill the aquarium or storage box two-thirds full of warm water. Pour the yeast into the cup or glass. Stir in the half teaspoon of sugar. Add the fourth cup of warm water and mix well. Scoop the soft yeast into one bottom corner of the plastic bag. Squeeze all the air out of the bag and seal. Rinse off the outside of the bag to be sure it's clean.

Place the bag on the bottom of the aquarium or clear storage box. Anchor it by setting the stone on top of the bag, but don't cover up the yeast mixture.

Check after fifteen minutes. Does the yeast look the same? In what way is the bag changing? Wait fifteen more minutes and check again. Surprise! By now, the bag should be floating at the surface.

Your experiment simulated what happens inside a dead fish. Each of the tiny yeast granules is a tiny plant that began to grow after you added water and sugar for food. As the yeast grew, it gave off gas that was trapped inside the bag, inflating it.

Most fish have a balloonlike sac, called a *swim bladder*, inside their body. Special body parts channel gas—mainly oxygen—from the fish's blood to this bladder. It's like blowing up a balloon except that the fish can control how much gas is in its swim bladder. More gas and the fish floats closer to the surface; less gas and it sinks.

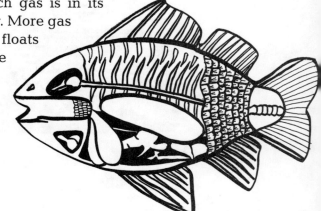

If a fish

happens to die when its swim bladder is full of gas, it naturally floats. If its swim bladder isn't full, the fish sinks, but it doesn't stay down. Bacteria, tiny living things, live in the fish's intestines, the long tube where food is digested. The bacteria help break down the food, but they give off gas in the process.

Although it's pretty icky to think about, people also have bacteria in their intestine, helping to break down food. That's why people pass gas. Living fish pass gas, too. In a dead fish, though, the gas stays inside the intestines and builds up. If enough gas builds up, the fish floats to the surface—belly-up because that's where its intestines are located.

The Truth About Slimy Animals—Maybe

While being slimy may seem disgusting to you, it's great for some animals. For example, clown fish coat themselves in mucous. This slime acts like a protective shield and lets them swim safely among the stinging tentacles of a slow-moving bottom-dwelling animal called a *sea anemone*. When other fish approach the clown fish resting among the tentacles, they're stung. Then the clown fish gets a meal and the sea anemone eats the leftovers. The young of the glowworm gnat (*Arachnocampa luminosa*) that's found only in caves in New Zealand, catches its food with long sticky strands of mucous it hangs from the ceiling. It has relatives in Australia that use this same sticky food-catching trick. The eggs of frogs and toads are coated in mucous to keep them from drying out. And earthworms can't breathe without a slimy mucous coat.

Want to find out more fascinating facts about slimy animals? Don't miss this quiz.

1) Snails and slugs give off mucous to coat their food before they eat it. True or False.

2) One kind of Australian frog survives long dry spells in its desert home by burying itself inside a mucous-lined bag. True or False.

3) Some salamanders have to be slimy to breathe. True or False.

4) Fish are slimy to keep them healthy. True or False.

5) When attacked, an octopus squirts slime at its enemy. True or False.

SOLUTIONS:

1) FALSE. Snails and slugs ooze mucous but they do it to create a slick carpet they can glide across. You may have discovered these winding, silver trails shimmering on a sidewalk. Snails and slugs eat by rasping off pieces of food, such as tomatoes and strawberries, with a special tooth-covered tongue.

2) TRUE. This Australian frog *(Cyclorana platycephalus)* buries itself, sheds its skin, and lines it with slimy mucous that it gives off from its new skin. When the shed skin dries it forms a tough waterproof bag. The moist mucous lining keeps the frog's skin moist. The frog's body stores water in its bladder, large water-holding nodes, and below its skin. As needed, this stored water moves

into the frog's blood and is transported throughout its body.

The frog may safely stay buried from a couple of months to as long as a year. When it rains, the frog comes out of its bag. The frogs only mate after a rain. Then the female frogs lay their eggs in puddles. The tadpoles quickly hatch and develop into frogs before the puddles dry up. The adults, new and old, bury themselves and wait inside their tough skin bags for the next rain.

3) TRUE. These salamanders lack lungs. Like you, though, they need oxygen from the air to live. Salamanders absorb oxygen through their skin, but this process only happens as long as their skin is moist. Then the oxygen is able to pass into a network of tiny blood vessels. From there the blood carries the oxygen through the salamander's body. Even frogs and toads and other types of salamanders that have lungs depend on their mucous-coated skin to deliver some of their oxygen needs.

4) TRUE. A coating of mucous protects fish from infections that could make them sick or even kill them. Being slimy also helps fish slip through the water more easily.

5) FALSE. When in danger, an octopus squirts out an inky substance in an octopus shape. This creates a decoy. With any luck the enemy attacks the ink, giving the octopus time to escape.

An Important Ingredient in Perfume Comes from a *Whale's* Gut?

It's true. A sperm whale's digestive system produces a waxy substance called *ambergris* that builds up into a lump. When dried, ambergris has a sweet seaweed scent. Nero's wife, Poppaea Sabina, was known to use oil of ambergris as a fragrance as early as A.D. 54. Ancient Arabs and Africans mixed ambergris that had been dried and ground into a powder with coffee and drank it to stimulate their heart. During the Middle Ages, ambergris was thought to be a cure for the plague. Then, during a period of history called the Renaissance, when people began to bathe more frequently and use perfumes, ambergris became really valuable. The artisans who mixed scents together to create perfume were often disappointed when the odors quickly changed. Adding ambergris fixed the scent, keeping it just the way it was originally created. As recently as the late 1960s, perfumers were paying several times the price of gold for ambergris.

So why does a sperm whale produce ambergris? While people used to believe it was the result of a disease or even constipation, it's now believed to be caused by eating squid. Sperm whales love to eat squid, but a squid has a sharp, hard beak the whale can't digest. If a number of these beaks poke into the whale's tender stomach or the intestinal wall, waxy ambergris is produced. This material coats the sharp beak, building up layer upon layer until the beak is buried and no longer an irritant. Scientists believe that all whales probably produce ambergris but that they periodically pass the lump. Some lumps can weigh hundreds of kilograms. Being oily, the ambergris floats on the sea. And while outer layers may dissolve or break off in the waves, if the lump is large enough some will be left to wash up on the beach. For many years, ambergris was bought from fishermen who scooped it out of the water or from beachcombers who found it on the shore. Later, whalers dug ambergris out of the whale carcass after the blubber was removed. Although this waxy material wasn't in every carcass, some of the lumps were huge. In 1912, a small whaling company found the largest lump of ambergris on record—455 kilograms (about 1,000 pounds). On the verge of bankruptcy at the time, the ambergris sale saved the company.

You Can Blow Up a Balloon with a Smashed Banana

This experiment calls for a smashed banana. So put a very ripe banana inside a self-sealing plastic bag, set the bag in the kitchen sink, and squash it with your hand. Do it again and again until the banana has been reduced to a mushy pulp. Now you can use the banana pulp and a process that just happens naturally to blow up a balloon.

You'll need:
- **10- to 12-ounce glass or plastic bottle with a small mouth**
- **half a ripe banana**
- **sturdy rubber balloon with a mouth big enough to fit over the drink bottle**
- **spoon**
- **fork**
- **plate**

Scoop the smashed banana into the clean, empty bottle. Slip the mouth of the balloon over the neck of the bottle. Set the bottle in a warm place and look at it once a day.

Bacteria, tiny living things, attack the banana. They use the banana's natural fruit sugar for food to grow and multiply, producing more bacteria. In the process, they give off gas. Usually, the gas escapes into the air, but now the gas is trapped inside the balloon. The more the banana rots, the more the balloon inflates. Of course, the balloon will never inflate as much as it would if you blew air into it.

Can any other squishy foods, such as grapes or plums, blow up a balloon? Can any make it inflate more than the banana?

You can design an experiment to find out. Try any foods you like, but remember to keep everything else about your test identical—bottles, balloons, amount of food used, and air temperature around the bottles. Then compare the amount of gas each food gives off by using a tape measure to determine which balloon is the biggest around. Be sure to measure each balloon at its fattest point.

Note: When you're finished testing, work in a sink or outdoors to remove the balloons. Throw the balloons away and wash out the bottles before recycling them. Be sure to wash your hands thoroughly, too.

Blow the Lid Off!

Would you believe that soup beans can pop the cap off a pill bottle? They can when they soak up water. Try this activity to find out how.

You'll need:
- **plastic pill bottle with a snap-on cap (do not use a childproof safety cap)**
- **bag of dry soup beans (available at grocery stores)**
- **water**

Pack the plastic pill bottle full of dry bean seeds so the top seeds are just below the rim. Next, add enough water to fill up all the spaces around the beans without spilling over. Snap on the cap. Let the bottle full of beans set overnight.

Surprise! In the morning, you'll discover the top has popped and beans are squishably soft. Wonder what happened? Take a close look at a dry bean. You'll see a tiny hole on the indented side. This hole lets water into the seed. The hard, starchy material that makes up the seed soaks up water. The tough seed coat is also softened by the water, allowing the seed to swell. This is actually the normal process that happens when a seed gets ready to sprout. The pressure exerted by all the swelling seeds at once, though, is enough to pop the top off the bottle. If the cap is too tight, the sides of the pill bottle might actually crack.

Which Has the Most Squish?

Oops! A full glass of red punch just spilled on your family's new carpeting. You could grab a handful of paper towels, a T-shirt, a cotton terry cloth towel, a wool sweater, or a polyester knit shirt. But since you have the same amount of each material within grabbing distance, which should you use? Which material will soak up the most punch? Try this experiment to find out.

You'll need:
- **identical 15-centimeter (about 6-inch) squares of an old T-shirt, paper towel, cotton terry cloth, wool, and polyester knit**
- **kitchen sink**
- **5 clear plastic cups**
- **red food coloring**
- **measuring cup**

Fill the sink half full of cool water and drip in enough food coloring to dye the water red. Push the squares underwater, making sure the materials don't overlap. If any material floats, anchor it with something, such as a rock, to hold it down. After five minutes, take the squares out and put one in each of the cups. Squeeze out the squares, one at a time, collecting the water in the cup. Stop squeezing when no more water flows out.

Compare the water levels. Which material appears to have soaked up more water? To find out exactly how much water each material captured, pour the water—one cup at a time—into the measuring cup. Write down the number of ounces each material soaked up. Repeat this test two more times and compare to make sure you got about the same results each time.

You should have discovered that the terry cloth soaked up the most water. This material gained its super absorbency from the fluffy loops. Each acted like a wick, drawing in and trapping the liquid. If you have a magnifying glass available, take a look at each of the test materials. You'll see that the materials that have a looser weave, meaning more spaces between the threads, and the materials that had fluffy fibers did a better job than those with a tight weave.

What other materials could you test to see if they will soak up even more water? Repeat the test with those materials.

Pet a Worm

The next time you see an earthworm crawling across the sidewalk, grab it. Or if you can't find any earthworms outdoors, purchase some from a store that sells fishing supplies and bait.

Does the earthworm feel squishy? It should. Worms lack a skeleton—the bones that give your body a shape. The worm will also feel slippery because its skin gives off mucous, the same sort of thick liquid that is produced in your nose. A mucous coating helps keep the worm moist—which lets it absorb the oxygen it needs to live through its skin. Stroke both sides of the worm with your fingers. Feel the tiny bristles sticking out of the worm's skin? These grip the ground, helping the worm push itself along.

Next, use a spray bottle to moisten a paper towel. Place the worm on the towel and mist it, too. Then watch as the worm moves. You move when your muscles pull on your bones. Since a worm lacks a skeleton, its body gets longer and thinner and then shorter and fatter as its muscles move.

Give your worm some obstacles to deal with, such as pebbles or clods of damp soil. How does the worm react when it runs into one of these obstacles?

Hold a worm race. Place four paper towels together. Use a Magic Marker to draw as big a circle as you can on the paper. Mist the paper so it's damp. Place several worms at the center of the circle. The first worm to crawl across the circle is the winner. Or for slow-moving crawlers, the closest to the circle in two minutes wins.

Build a Worm Farm

Since earthworms are normally underground, you usually can't see them in their tunnels. But build an earthworm farm and you can watch these icky, squishy critters in action.

You'll need:
- **clean, clear 2-liter plastic soft drink bottle**
- **scissors**
- **masking tape**
- **5 centimeters (about 2 inches) square of new sponge**
- **black construction paper**
- **measuring cup**
- **mesh bag, such as one potatoes come in**
- **2 cups grass clippings or crumbled dry leaves**
- **enough good garden soil or potting soil to nearly fill 2-liter bottle**

Cut the top off the bottle five centimeters below the neck. Cut a sheet out of the mesh bag, or panty hose, big enough to cover the top of the bottle. Tape the black paper to form a tube a little taller than the bottle and big enough around so that it will slide on easily. Fill the bottle nearly full of soil. Add the grass clippings or crumbled leaves and mix in enough water to make the soil feel damp, but not soggy. Soak the sponge in water, squeeze it out, and place it on top of the soil.

Collect the earthworms for your farm after a heavy rain. They come out onto the surface when their tunnels collapse or fill with water. Or buy them. Because your worm farm is small, only stock about six worms.

Gently pick up a worm with damp hands. Put the worms into their new home and cover them with grass clippings or leaves. The worms need air so cover the top of the worm farm with the mesh, securing it with tape. Place the worm farm in a cool place out of direct sunlight. Slide the black tube over the bottle. Earthworms live underground most of the time, and they like it dark.

Every few days check to be sure the sponge is damp. After a week, feed your worms shredded bits of grass, lettuce, or potato peelings by leaving these on the surface. After two days, replace any moldy food with fresh food.

After a week slide off the paper tube and take a look. The worms will have created tunnels through the soil. Are more of the tunnels near the top, middle, or bottom of the farm? Earthworms create their tunnels by eating their way through the soil. And their wastes contain broken-down plant material that enriches the soil with materials that help plants grow. Earthworms also help plants grow by pushing apart soil grains. It's easier for plant roots to push through this loosened soil. And water and oxygen move more easily

down into the soil through these spaces between soil grains. Plants need to take in oxygen and water through their roots to grow and stay healthy.

After a couple of weeks, find a nice garden spot to turn your captive worms loose. You may be surprised to learn that an acre of fertile land may be home to as many as a million earthworms.

Go on a Polymer Hunt

Once there was the Stone Age. Then there was the Bronze Age. Today, you're living in the Polymer Age. Polymers are all around you—in the fabric your clothes are made of, the base for the gum you chew, the film you load into your camera, and in lots more everyday items.

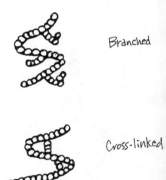

Polymers start with molecules, those tiny building blocks that make up everything. Molecules just naturally occur singly. Sometimes, though, molecules link together into chains of similar molecules. Then they're called *polymers*, from "poly," meaning many, and "mer," meaning members. There are natural polymers like paper, silk, and rubber. And there are synthetic polymers, created when scientists make chains of molecules hook together.

Synthetic polymers were invented as substitutes for expensive natural polymers, but later more were created as special materials with unique traits. One of the first synthetic polymers, *celluloid*, was produced by John Wesley Hyatt in 1868. Celluloid was created to use instead of ivory for making billiard balls. Celluloid was less expensive to produce and easier to obtain than killing elephants for their ivory tusks. Celluloid also didn't have to be carved. It could easily be molded into shapes that then hardened. Early movie films were celluloid. Since this synthetic polymer was flammable, movie theaters kept buckets of sand next to the projector to smother the flames if the film caught on fire.

In 1884 another polymer was invented as a substitute for an expensive, difficult to obtain material—silk. The synthetic was called artificial silk but it was really a form of rayon. In 1938 Wallace Carothers produced an even more important synthetic polymer—nylon. When nylon stockings first went on sale in 1940 nearly four million pairs were sold in just four days.

But it was World War II that made synthetic polymers

essential. Suddenly, a supply of rubber for truck, tank, and airplane tires was cut off because it came from tropical countries that were inaccessible to the U.S. So scientists developed synthetic rubber that turned out to have even better qualities than the real thing. After the war, scientists set to work producing even more synthetic materials made of polymers.

Now it's time for you to find some of the many polymers that are all around you. Here are the names of just a few of the many polymers you might discover: polystyrene, polyvinyl chloride, Lucite, Kevlar, polyethylene, Antron, Teflon, fluoropolymers, polyacetal, Glyptal, Dacron, polyester, Bakelite, and melamine. Copy the list of synthetic polymers and take it with you to a department store that carries a variety of items. Then check the labels and boxes for these polymers. Make a mark next to the polymer's name each time you discover something made from it. Which kind of polymer did you find used most often? What kinds of products, such as clothes, household products, and toys were made from each kind of polymer? If you have trouble identifying the polymers listed above, just look for things you recognize as made of a familiar polymer—plastic. How many different kinds of things can you find that are made of plastic?

Make Your Own Marshmallows

Ready to whip up a really icky, squishy treat you can eat? Then follow the recipe to make some marshmallows. Marshmallows are really a squishy polymer gel, a semirigid material made up of a random network of crystals with liquid filling up any spaces. Then the gel is whipped—forcing air into the spaces. The result is marshmallow cream that becomes marshmallows when shaped and allowed to dry.

What you'll be following, though, is the modern, Polymer Age recipe for marshmallows. Originally, what people called marshmallows wouldn't seem like a sweet treat to you. Those early marshmallows were made from the roots of mallow plants that grew in marshes. To make the yummy, modern version of marshmallows, just follow the recipe.

RECIPE COURTESY OF ANITA REED, UNIVERSITY OF GEORGIA COLLEGE OF AGRICULTURE EXTENSION AGENT.

You'll need:
- **metal mixing bowl**
- **measuring spoons**
- **measuring cup**
- **spoon**
- **rubber spatula**
- **saucepan with lid**
- **candy thermometer**

- **electric mixer**
- **timer**
- **oven mitt**
- **three 1/4-ounce envelopes unflavored gelatin**
- **2 cups granulated sugar**
- **3/4 cup light corn syrup**
- **2 tablespoons vanilla**
- **1 cup cornstarch**
- **cookie sheet**
- **quart size self-sealing plastic storage bag**

You'll need to use the stove, so ask an adult to be your partner and follow the directions carefully to stay safe.

Pour a half cup of cold water into the bowl. Sprinkle on the gelatin. Stir to mix. Let stand for one hour.

Meanwhile, lightly dust the cookie sheet with cornstarch. After about thirty minutes, begin to prepare the sugar syrup. Pour the sugar and corn syrup into the pan. Stir over low heat on the stove until the syrup begins to boil. Put the lid on and let cook for three minutes. This allows any sugar crystals that have formed on the sides of the pan to wash down into the syrup. Remove the lid and continue to cook without stirring. Place the bulb end of the candy thermometer in the hot syrup and watch until the temperature reaches 118°C (244°F). Have your adult partner pour the hot syrup slowly over the gelatin while you whip it with the mixer. Continue beating for ten minutes. Add the vanilla, beating again for a minute.

Dust the spoon with cornstarch. Scoop a spoonful of the mixture onto the cookie sheet. Repeat dusting and scooping until you've made at least two dozen marshmallows. Set the cookie sheet aside. The marshmallows need to set about twenty-four hours.

To store your homemade marshmallows, put one-fourth cup of cornstarch into a self-sealing plastic bag, seal, shake, and dump out any excess. Drop the marshmallows in a few at a time and shake to coat in cornstarch. Transfer dusted marshmallows to another bag.

Blow Up a Marshmallow!

What do you suppose will happen when you bombard a marshmallow with microwaves—those invisible rays that blast anything inside the oven when you switch the microwave on. Just follow the steps below to find out.

You'll need:
- **marshmallow**
- **juice glass**
- **paper towel**
- **scissors**
- **microwave oven**

You'll need to use the microwave, so ask an adult to be your partner and follow the directions carefully to stay safe.

Put one of your marshmallows in a juice glass, cover with a piece of paper towel just a little bigger than the top of the glass, and microwave for thirty seconds. Watch through the oven window so you won't miss the action.

Surprise! The marshmallow puffs up. Marshmallows, as you know, contain water molecules. When the water molecules are struck by microwaves, they vibrate wildly, producing heat—enough to change the water to steam. Trapped by the stretchy sugar molecules, the steam makes the marshmallows swell. Eventually though, all the steam escapes and the marshmallow collapses.

43

Now, heat a cup of cocoa in the microwave and top with the creamy, blown-up marshmallow.

Make a Catapult

What would happen if wars were fought with weapons that only shot marshmallows? Imagine planes dropping bombs of squishy marshmallows. Or guns shooting out bouncy marsh-mallow bullets. It certainly would be messy! Unfortunately, wars today aren't fought with marshmallows. But you can launch marshmallows using a weapon the ancient Romans and Greeks used to attack cities—a catapult.

Not sure what a catapult is? It's a device something like a seesaw. When one end is suddenly lowered the other end quickly rises, tossing up anything perched on its side. You may have seen acrobats in the circus use a catapult to toss someone up to the top of a tower of people. Or if you've ever watched a movie about the ancient Romans or Greeks attacking a city, you've probably seen a catapult in action. It could hurl big stones over high fortress walls and sling burning straw onto castle rooftops. A smaller version developed for Alexander the Great could be carried aboard a ship, increasing a navy's fighting power. Catapults are still used aboard aircraft carriers today. These machines launch airplanes from the ship's deck.

You won't be going to battle, but you can have fun exploring how a catapult works

by building one and launching marshmallows. When the catapult releases the marshmallow, you'll see it take an arching path through the air. This path is called its *trajectory*. In order to shoot your catapult accurately and hit a target, you'll need to pay attention to how the marshmallow's trajectory changes when the slope of the catapult is changed.

Now, collect the building materials you'll need and follow the directions.

You'll need:
- **30-centimeter (about 12-inch) long section of a 2-by-4 wood board**
- **electrician's tape or other strong tape**
- **sturdy plastic spoon**
- **6 marshmallows**
- **masking tape**
- **measuring tape or meter stick**
- **enough books to make a stack about 8 centimeters (about 3 inches) high**
- **safety goggles**

Because you will be launching objects—even though they're marshmallows—always wear safety goggles during tests. Have an adult partner work with you and choose a safe test site free of obstacles. Check before each launch to be sure no people are standing or sitting in the test area.

Place the spoon at one end of the board. Center it with the tip of the handle—about three centimeters (about one and a half inches)—on the board. Be sure the bowl of the spoon is facing up. Anchor the spoon with a strip of tape. Secure by tightly wrapping more tape around the board. Make a loop of masking tape—sticky side out—small enough to fit in the bowl of the spoon. Press it into the bowl of the spoon. Stack the books. Lean the board against the stack to form a gently sloping ramp. Place the marshmallow on the bowl of the spoon. Position yourself beside the catapult without leaning over it. Pull down gently but firmly on the bowl of the spoon and then let go.

As the spoon springs back, the marshmallow is launched into the air. Pushing past air molecules slows the marshmallow. Gravity, the force that pulls everything on the earth toward the ground, slows it, too. When the marshmallow is no longer traveling fast enough to resist gravity, it falls. Seen together, the marshmallow's soaring and falling creates its arching path—its trajectory. With the catapult sloping gently, the marshmallow's trajectory is a long, rainbow-shaped curve.

Copy the catapult test chart below and fill in the distance from the catapult to where the marshmallow landed. Do two more trials and record those distances, too. Replace the tape loop as needed to hold the marshmallow in position for launch. Next, add all three distances together and divide by three to get the average distance the marshmallow traveled when the catapult was sloping gently.

Catapult Test

Ramp Position	Trial 1	Trial 2	Trial 3
Average			
Gently sloping			
Steeply sloping			

Next, prop up the catapult so it is steeply sloping and launch a marshmallow. This time the ascent and descent will be steep, creating a trajectory shaped like a narrow arched doorway. Measure how far the marshmallow traveled and record this distance on the chart. Do two more trials and compute an average.

Now compare the results produced by the two ramp positions. You can see that if you want to launch something that will go a long distance, you'll need to use a gently sloping catapult. To have something go farther up into the air and drop closer to the ramp, you need to make the catapult ramp steeply sloping.

Just for fun, see if you can use the catapult to accurately hit a target. Draw a circle on the ground or use a large mixing bowl as your target. Set the catapult one and a half meters (about five feet) from the target. Position the catapult so the marshmallow lands on your target. If you don't hit the target on the first try, adjust your catapult and try again.

How Long Does the Flavor Really Last?

One of the ickiest things you can have in your mouth is a wad of old chewing gum after the flavor is gone. The flavor starts to disappear the instant you put a piece of chewing gum into your mouth. Saliva, the natural juice in your mouth, washes off the sugary coating. Then, as you chew, saliva dissolves the sweet flavoring. It won't dissolve the gum base, though, and eventually all you're left with is a disgusting, rubbery lump. So how long does chewing gum taste good? And does one brand of gum stay tasty longer than another? Try this activity to find out.

You'll need:
- **3 sticks of three different brands of sugar-free gum (all need to be the same flavor for the best comparison)**
- **clock**

Minutes Flavor Lasts

Brand	Prediction	Test 1	Test 2	Test 3	Average

Copy the chart above to record your results. Based on your past experience or advertisements you've seen, predict how long you think the flavor will last for each brand of gum. For the results to be compared, everything about the test should be the same except the brands of gum. So make a list of the things you'll need to do to keep the tests identical. You'll undoubtedly think of others, but start with these:

1) chewing with the same force;
2) chewing on both sides of your mouth;
3) keeping your mouth closed during chewing.

When you're ready to start testing, wash your hands and put one piece of gum in your mouth.

You'll have to judge carefully when the flavor is gone because some types of chewing gum have a lingering aftertaste. To give each brand a fair evaluation, test just one brand a day. That way your judgment won't be affected by tired jaws.

To figure the average number of minutes the flavor lasted for one brand, add together the total number of minutes from the three tests. Then divide this total by three. How close was this average to your prediction?

An especially elastic material is one of the ingredients in bubble gum's base. So bubble gum can be stretched more easily to blow bubbles. But will some brands of bubble gum let you blow bigger bubbles more easily than others? Think about it. Then plan a test to find out. Check with an adult to be sure your test idea is safe for you to perform. Then carry out your test. Why will you need to test each brand of bubble gum at least three times?

Remember to dispose of all chewed gum as you would any solid waste.

What Is in Chewing Gum?

You may be surprised to learn that what makes chewing gum chewy is pretty disgusting stuff. Chewing gum is mainly an elastic material called *gum base*. That's the stuff that you spit out when the flavor is gone and you're tired of chewing.

Dinah Diaz, product development chemist for the gum base manufacturer L.A. Dreyfus Company, reports that today gum base is usually a synthetic rubber polymer called *butadiene styrene*. This is blended with another chewing material, such as petroleum wax or polyvinyl acetate. To make chewing gum, the gum base is heated in large kettles to about 115°C (240°F). This makes it the consistency of pancake syrup. Next, the base moves on to huge mixers with slowly rotating paddles. Powdered sugar, corn syrup, and flavorings are added. Then the gum passes along cooling belts and through extruders, machines that change it into sticks, chunks, and balls. The finished gum is dusted with a powdery coating of sugar or a nonsugar sweetener to keep the pieces from sticking together or to the wrapper.

Chewing gum is nothing new. The ancient Greeks chewed *mastiche*, resin from the mastic tree. People in the Middle East chewed mastic resin combined with beeswax, which made it softer and easier to chew. The ancient Mayans were the first to chew "chicle," the sap from the Mexican sapodilla tree. This material was the basic stuff chewing gum was made of until the synthetic polymers were invented. In New England, Native Americans and early settlers chewed the resin from spruce trees. Before 1899, chewing gum wasn't especially tasty stuff. Then William White, whose company produced Chiclets, discovered a way to add flavoring to chewing gum.

Make Fake Amber

Tree sap is icky and messy if you get it on you, but it's good for the tree. The sap that oozes out of a crack in the bark forms a sort of Band-Aid. It seals out bugs and fungi that could harm the tree. There's been sticky sap oozing out of cracks and holes in cone-bearing trees, such as pine trees and spruce trees, since ancient times. When this sap dries and becomes golden yellow and rock hard it's called *amber*. Unlike real rocks, amber can burn, giving off a pine scent. Sometimes it also provides glimpses of the past because leaves or seeds or insects get stuck in the sap. These are preserved and protected from bacteria that could make them decay. To see how bits of past life become preserved in amber, perform this activity.

You'll need:
- **an old pencil**
- **clear nail polish**
- **tweezers**
- **small seed, such as a small unpopped popcorn kernel**
- **old newspapers**
- **old paintbrush**

Cover your work area with newspapers. Set the pencil on the newspapers. Drip a drop of the clear polish on the pencil. The pencil is your tree branch and the polish is the sap. Use the tweezers to place the seed on the drop of polish. The seed will sink and be engulfed by the polish. If it doesn't, add more clear nail polish on top of the seed. Depending on the drying speed of the polish, it should quickly set, becoming hard within an hour. Wait overnight, though, to let it completely harden.

Real tree sap becomes rock-hard amber much more slowly. And this process is still going on. Go outdoors and search for modern amber in the making. You'll need to check cone-bearing trees, like pines and spruce trees. Can you find sap droplets where they've oozed out and collected on the bark? If an insect lands on it and sinks into the sap, it could become preserved. Then one day scientists might examine it to learn about life in the past.

Did You Know that Bad Breath *Isn't* Caused by Food Odors in Your Mouth?

Your breath may smell bad after you eat onions or garlic, but your mouth isn't to blame. Onions and garlic contain oils that are absorbed by the digestive system and passed on to the bloodstream. Then the oils are transported by the blood to the lungs. There the oils mix with the carbon dioxide gas you just naturally exhale, producing bad-smelling breath.

When it's your mouth that really *does* smell bad, the problem is called *halitosis*. These odors are the result of not brushing your teeth, tooth decay, or gum disease. To solve this problem, you need to brush regularly or be treated by a dentist or a periodontist, a doctor who treats gum disease.

Use Your Mighty Breath!

You have probably been told that you breathe in oxygen, a gas that's in the air, and that you breathe out another gas called *carbon dioxide*. Carbon dioxide gas is just naturally given off as waste when your body combines oxygen and the food you eat to produce energy. Of course, you can't actually see the oxygen going into your body or the carbon dioxide going out because these gases are odorless and invisible. But you can use the carbon dioxide you puff out to cause a chemical reaction—and *that* you can see.

You'll need:
- **phenol red (inexpensive and available at pool supply stores)**
- **quart jar**
- **clean straw**
- **safety goggles**

Fill the quart jar about two-thirds full of cool tap water. Add twenty drops of phenol red or enough to make the water light red. Put on your goggles.

Put the straw in the water and blow bubbles for twenty seconds. The water should already look less red, but repeat blowing for twenty seconds two more times. By the time you finish blowing for the third time, the water should be clear. If it isn't, continue blowing into the water until it is.

This color change from red to clear happens because phenol red is an indicator, meaning that it changes to show the presence of certain substances called acids. You already discovered the properties of acids when you made a chicken bone bend (page 7). This time the carbon dioxide you blew out reacted with the water to produce a weak acid. As soon as the acid level in the water was high enough to cause a reaction, the phenol red changed, becoming clear.

Sometimes carbon dioxide from burning gasoline or coal can cause rainwater to be a weak acid. This may damage plants. It can also cause the surface of sculptures or other things made of stone to erode a tiny bit. You may have noticed that old sculptures sometimes have features that are hard to make out or that writing carved into stone (like tombstones) seems to be worn away.

Watch Out for Sticky Plants!

In horror movies, evil or alien plants sometimes strangle people. Some even eat people. Can plants really be so nasty? To reach Sleeping Beauty, the prince had to chop his way through prickly vines that had grown over the castle. Do vines ever use their thorns to help them climb? To find the answers to these plant questions and more, take this quiz.

1) The strangler fig got its name because it's a serial killer. True or False.

2) Some vines use thorns to help themselves climb. True or False.

3) Slime molds are plants that look like the jellylike white of an egg that's been colored white, yellow, or gray. And they can move. True or False.

4) The seeds of some plants hitch rides to move to a new location. True or False.

5) Sundews are alien-looking plants that sometimes catch and eat people. True or False.

SOLUTIONS:

1) FALSE. Each strangler fig kills only once, and luckily its victim is a tree. A strangler fig starts its jungle life when a bird or bat happens to deposit its seed on a bit of decaying plant matter high in a tree. The seed sprouts and the young plant sends roots down along the tree's trunk. Its stem and leaves climb up to the sunshine. Because the strangler fig grows quickly, more and more roots and stems spread around the tree's trunk. Finally, the tree's supply of food and water is cut off and it dies. The strangler fig is now strong and independent.

2) TRUE. Some, like bougainvillea and rambler roses, have thorns that catch on anything they touch. This keeps the vine from sliding backward as the plant climbs. Giant rattan plants, the kind used to make rattan furniture, have thorny whiplike parts. These thrash around until they snag onto something. Then, using this support, the rattan climbs higher. Still another tropical rain forest plant called *Quisqualis* climbs by grabbing onto any available support with hooks that develop on its branches and leaves.

60

3) TRUE. Scientists call slime mold *Mycetozoa*, meaning "fungus animal," because it acts a little like both plants and animals. Like an animal, slime mold moves, but you probably won't notice this action because it happens very slowly—as slow as cold honey pouring out of a bottle. So it becomes clear only over time that the slime mold has changed position, creeping down the side of a rotting log, for example. Related to bread mold and mushrooms, slime mold gets the nutrients it needs from the rotting plant material it moves across. At some point, the slime mold stops moving and produces tiny stalks called *sporangium*—each topped by a delicate ball full of seedlike spores. The spores are carried away by the wind. If they land in a moist spot where conditions are right, they grow into a new slime mold and begin to travel again.

4) TRUE. Sticktights, which are sometimes called *beggar-ticks*, are just one type of seed that hitches a ride. These seeds have two sharp prongs to cling to an animal's fur as it brushes past. You may have gotten some of these or other sticky seeds caught on your socks or pant legs. If the seed comes free and lands where conditions are right, it will sprout and a new plant will grow. Mistletoe is another plant whose seeds hitch a ride. But these seeds are coated in a natural glue. When a bird eats mistletoe berries, the seeds stick to its beak. Later, if the bird wipes its beak against a tree's bark, the seeds settle on the bark, sprout, and begin to grow.

5) FALSE. These strange-looking plants catch and eat animals, but people are never on the menu. Sundews primarily eat insects. These plants live in bogs and can make their own food. But the soil is so poor, they can't get all the nutrients they need to grow and produce seeds. These extra nutrients come from the animals it eats. To catch these meals, the plant spreads spoon-size leaves studded with dozens of short tentacles—each topped with a sticky drop of liquid. When an insect lands on a leaf, it's likely to get stuck. Next, digestive juices ooze out of the leaf, slowly breaking down the insect. Then the plant absorbs the nutrient "soup" that's produced. The wind blows away any hard parts that couldn't be digested. Other plants, like the Venus flytrap and the pitcher plant, also catch insects to get the nutrients they need.

This Could Get Squishy!

You probably think you know what will happen when you turn a glass full of water upside down. But you're in for a big surprise—thanks to science.

You'll need:
- **sturdy plastic cup**
- **sturdy paper plate**
- **paper towel**

Because this trick could get messy, wear old clothes and get an adult's permission. You'll also want to work outdoors or over the kitchen sink.

Fill the plastic cup nearly full of water. Fold the paper towel into fourths and place it on the middle of the plate. Next, turn the plate and towel over the cup like a lid. Hold the plate against the top of the cup with your fingers while you turn the whole system over.

Now the cup is on top. Be sure it is straight up and down. Hold on to the cup with the hand that isn't pressing up on the plate. Then—slowly—take your hand away from the plate. The plate shouldn't fall and the water should stay inside the glass.

What's holding the plate in place? It's air! Even though it's invisible, air has weight and takes up space. Air is also all around you, so it exerts force on you and objects and other people from all directions. As gravity pulls down on the water inside the glass a partial vacuum is created in the air-filled space inside the jar. Now the downward force of the water and air inside the glass is less than all the upward pushing force of air on the plate. You can see how much larger this surface is than that covered by the water inside the glass. The wet paper towel helps by making a tight seal between the glass and the plate. This keeps any air from slipping inside the glass. If that happened, the air rushing into the glass would push the water out. Then there would be a flood and you'd get wet.

Shoot Water Without a Squirt Gun!

Ready for more squishy fun? Then try this to make a jet of water shoot into the air all by itself.

You'll need:
- **candle in a holder**
- **matches**
- **4-penny nail**
- **oven mitt**
- **2-liter plastic bottle**
- **masking tape**
- **safety goggles (for you and your adult partner)**

You'll need to use a flame, so work with an adult partner and follow the directions carefully to stay safe.

After you both put on your safety goggles, have your adult partner light the candle. Then have your adult partner use the oven mitt to hold the sharp nail tip in the flame for a few seconds. Next, your partner should press the hot nail tip straight into the middle of the plastic bottle. The nail will melt a hole—turning the nail will help enlarge the hole slightly. Then have your partner reheat the nail to make two more holes—one about five centimeters (about two inches) above the first hole and another about five centimeters (about two inches) below it.

Cover the holes with tape and place the bottle in the sink. Let a slow steady stream of water run into the bottle to fill it. Place the bottle on the counter next to the sink with the tape side toward the sink. Peel off the tape.

Surprise! Water shoots out all three holes. This happens because air moving into the bottle pushes the water out. Any air bubbles you see in the water are evidence of this. You may be surprised to see that the water shoots out the bottom hole farther than it does from the other two holes. Water has weight. The weight of the water pushing down makes the pressure greatest at the bottom of the column of water inside the bottle. The stronger the pressure the stronger the water jet. You may have felt the water pressure change in your ears when you dived toward the bottom of a swimming pool. Watch what happens to the water jets as the water level in the bottle goes down, decreasing the amount of water pressure.

What Caused These Icky, Sticky Events?

Extremely bad storms, earthquakes, volcanic eruptions —the earth isn't always a peaceful place to live. Some-times, as in these three examples, the results of what's happening on the earth—or under it—can be icky and sticky. Read what happened and then brainstorm. Make a list of all the things you think could have caused each event. Then read the solutions to find out what in the world really happened.

1) On May 8, 1981, the earth suddenly began to sink in the front yard of a house in Winter Park, Florida. Within twenty-four hours the hole had become as wide as half a football field and deeper than a three story building. Why did this hole suddenly appear? And why at that particular spot?

2) On the night of September 12, 1977, Brush Creek near Kansas City, Kansas, suddenly rose nearly seven meters (twenty-two feet). Then, roaring with the force of a mighty river, it crashed through restaurants, swept away cars, and killed twenty-five people. What made this little trickling creek turn into a raging river?

3) The little horse was running flat out but the saber-toothed cat was closing in fast. Suddenly the horse slammed to a stop, whinnying. The cat leaped, landing on the horse. As though realizing this was a mistake the cat struggled to spring away, but it was too late. The two animals were stuck in a lake of sticky black tar. Nearly ten thousand years later, the fossil remains of these animals and hundreds of others have been carefully removed from the tar lake at La Brea, near Los Angeles, California. So far more than 500 different kinds of animals, including insects, have been found well-preserved by a coating of tar that hardened into asphalt. But how did this lake of tar form? And why did so many animals become trapped in the sticky stuff?

SOLUTIONS:

1)	The hole that suddenly appeared in Winter Park, Florida, is called a *sinkhole*. Under the grass and soil everyone could see on the earth's surface, the city was built on top of limestone. This is a type of rock that naturally dissolves as rainwater soaks down through it. In fact, Winter Park was built on the roof of a huge cave filled with water. The city's water supply was the water in this cave. So as the town's population grew, water was drawn out of this cave faster than new rainwater could soak in to replace it. The water level in the cave was a lot lower after a drought, a long period without rain. Then without the water to help support the weight of the town, the cave roof collapsed. Winter Park chose not to fill in its sinkhole and rebuild. Instead, the town turned the hole into a public lake.

2)	What happened to Brush Creek was a *flash flood*. Anytime a lot of water drains into a stream, it's likely to flood. And when this happens suddenly, the flood flows downstream in a powerful wave. On September 11, 1977, Kansas City, Kansas, got six inches of rain—an unusually heavy amount. Then on September 12, another seven inches of rain fell in just six hours. So much water falling in so little time meant very little had time to soak into the ground. Most drained off, running into Brush Creek. To make matters worse, years before the flash flood a corrupt city official who owned a cement company paved four miles of Brush Creek's bed with concrete at the city's expense. So the floodwater shot through the paved section of the creek the way it would through a pipe. It was estimated that by the time the water struck the restaurant it was traveling at a speed of six meters (twenty feet) per second—fast enough to smash through the building and send cars tumbling. Flash floods remain among the hardest weather disasters to predict and among the most damaging worldwide.

3) The tar lake that trapped the horse and saber-toothed cat formed when oil from large deposits underground rose to the surface through cracks. As some of the liquid part of the oil evaporated, it became thicker and stickier, forming tar. Then rains formed pools on top of the sticky tar and leaves floated on the surface of the water. Animals couldn't see the tar until they had walked into the sticky stuff. Then they couldn't get out. Insects and birds also landed and got stuck. Some of the most unusual animal remains that have been found include a huge ground sloth, a kind of camel, and a giant bird called Merriam's teratorn. This extinct bird, relative of today's storks, had a four-meter (fourteen-foot) wingspan.